Praise for Troy James Weaver & Selected Stories

"There's just something weirdly perfect about Troy James Weaver's stories. Perfect because they are, down to their syllables. Weird because what they do feels so broken it hurts. It's a kind of double whammy effect, part awe, part ache, that's truly singular as far as I know."

    —Dennis Cooper, author of The Marbled Swarm

"I don't like telling people what to do and I don't like being told what to do. But right now I'm telling you to read the stories of Troy James Weaver. From the beginning, Weaver's been unafraid to show us humanity in all its grotesque, stupid, and beautiful glory. His stories are for the young and for the old, for the strong and the weak, for the sick and the dying and the dead. Luckily, if you're reading this, you're alive and you're holding this book in your hands. Read these stories and learn a little bit about what it means to be alive."

    —Joseph Grantham, author Raking Leaves

SELECTED STORIES

TROY JAMES WEAVER

APOCALYPSE PARTY

Selected Stories

Versions of some of these stories were previously published by *New York Tyrant Magazine*, *X-R-A-Y Magazine*, *Hobart*, *Sprung Formal*, and *Faded Out*.

ISBN-13: 978-1-7335694-2-2
ISBN-10: 1-7335694-2-1

Cover design by Matthew Revert

www.apocalypse-party.com

First Edition

Printed in the U.S.A

Sound Check

Is this thing on?

CONTENTS

INTRODUCTION

Here we go. The best Troy James Weaver stories collected together in one place. This is cause for celebration. What you've got in your hands may feel like a paperback book but it's actually a gold brick worth $360,000 right now, if you ask me.

Every once in a while an artist like Weaver comes along and it wakes me up, gets me going, and I thank my lucky stars.

These stories were written at a warehouse full of flowers, on the backs of order forms, during lunch breaks taken in a half-broken down car out there in the dust and the sunshine.

Troy works for a living, and there's no such thing as an ordinary day for him.

He's taken a piece of the sky and made art with it for you. He's taken a rose and pricked his finger and put his blood in the art for you too. He even threw in the rose.

Where did he come from? Kansas. Who are his people? You are. What is he saying? Everything.

Troy James Weaver is one of the greatest American writers if you ask me. I hold him right up there with Raymond Carver, Lydia Davis, Scott McClanahan, Joy Williams.

Well, enjoy this brick of gold. It's full of beauty and pain, ugliness and holiness, sorrow and joy. When I said it was worth $360,000 I was just kidding around. It's priceless, that's what it is. Priceless.

—Bud Smith

CONSTRUCTION

The rooms they rented near the pipeline were these cheap, one-night-stand affairs—a twin bed, a tiny TV, a fridge made for a college dorm, cigarette burns in the sheets, the smell of sweat and ancient milk, souring in the tepid, stale air—and there were occasional power failures, too, which happened at least once every two weeks. Kit was late getting up and into the field on mornings like that. Everybody else made it just fine—Ed, Chris, even Tito. They would already be there, dirtied from head to toe, readying themselves to give Kit shit as he walked up over the crunching gravel from his tiny pickup truck—and this particular day started off no different than the others.

"You were hitting it hard last night, eh?" Ed tucked dip under his lip and grinned.

Tito laughed. "Guess it was the power again, huh? Doesn't your bitch-ass have a cellphone?"

Ignoring them, Kit strapped his helmet on and sipped coffee from his Thermos, thinking about how much he didn't want to think about anything anymore—how if he could just make it through the day, he could forget everything again come nightfall.

It'd been a little over a year now since his son had taken off and vanished into the wild, uncomfortable depths of the world. He always thought of him, even when he tried to deaden it with things, but he never mourned him. He still had some fervent, undying hope in his gut that the kid would come walking up out of nowhere one day and say, *Dad? Is that you? Dad? I've been looking for you. It's me. Tanner.*

They worked for hours under the scorching sun—the others trying to remember while Kit tried to forget.

Not long after lunch, Tito and Ed observed Kit about a hundred yards off, digging frantically in the dirt, just gouging and punching and scraping like a dog. They both watched for a minute before they started off in his direction. When they got over there, he was saying, "Yes, yes, yes. I saved him. Look he's still breathing. Look at this thing. He's still alive. Can you believe it? I can hardly believe he's still alive."

"What the fuck," said Ed. "You need to drink some water."

"Look at this," said Kit. "He's still alive. It's a miracle. I saw his little grey arm sticking up. He was buried alive."

Tito appeared to be distressed, kept chewing at his lip, grinding his teeth, and would hardly hold Kit's gaze as he reached down to help him to his feet. "Come on, kid. You need to take a break. Heat's getting to you."

"What're you talking about?" Kit was about to light a cigarette. Tito knocked it clean out of his hand. "Holy shit, I'm so sorry. Forgot where I was for a second."

"Come on," they said.

When they got back to the lunch trailer, they sat Kit in front of a fan and got him some water.

"Look at this, can you believe it. I saved this fucker. Isn't he beautiful? I can't believe he's still alive."

"Jesus, Kit," said Ed. "It's just a toy, an alien, a plush toy."

Kit hardly paid attention to what Ed was saying, instead he just kept going, "I can hardly believe he's still alive. I can hardly believe he's still alive."

Ed and Tito sat there a minute, darting glances back and forth, and then whispered to each other. Ed went out and told the foreman that Kit wasn't feeling too good and needed to take the rest of the day off. Tito stayed behind to tell Kit he needed to go back to the hotel and get some rest.

Kit nodded and said, "Isn't it so great?"

"Yeah," said Tito. "It's a miracle. Now, go on. You have the rest of the day off. Take advantage of it."

"All right," said Kit. "See you guys."

Before he left, he tried to give it a drink of water. It dribbled off the stiff grey cloth and onto his jeans, made a spot like urine that spread over his lap and into his skin. As he walked back to his truck, Chris waved, trying to get his attention, a sad look in his eyes, but he didn't notice and just kept walking, dust kicking up and stirring ghostly off each step.

He buckled the plush alien into the passenger seat of his pickup and made his way back to the hotel, the sky turning from a hot bright summer blue into a hard slate grey as a storm rolled in over top the particular patch of earth he was driving on.

At his room, Kit washed the plush alien in the sink, cut off the tag, and used a blow dryer to dry it off. He closed the toilet lid and sat it down there. He turned on the hot water, got a shower going, climbed in after peeling off his clothes, and said, "What's your name?" He waited, one ear cupped, while water ran down his face, straining to listen. "Well, that's okay. You're probably still feeling weak. You've been through hell and back, surely. I'll let it come as it comes. Hope you don't mind, you know, but that thing sticking out of you didn't look all that comfortable so I cut it off." He listened for anything, a stir, but heard nothing, especially with all that water beating into him.

He stayed up the rest of the day watching cartoons with the plush alien beside him on the bed. He popped the occasional pill and chased it with whiskey. Hours and hours went by like this until nighttime slowly covered the windows with its lightless mold. He stumbled outside and sat on a parking block, plush alien in hand. He'd tried talking to it all day to no avail. He was feeling restless, resentful—angry that the thing would disrespect him like that and after all he'd done. Not even one *Thank you.*

"Listen, kid," he said. "You need to tell me your name." He smoked a cigarette and counted the stars. Several minutes passed. He kept touching the alien's wrist and telling it to say something, anything. He felt he was owed something, even though he wanted something more than that. "Come on, say something, anything. Say it, just fucking say something." He was surprised that he seemed to be yelling, but embraced it, emboldened it. "Fuck you," he said. He threw the alien on the pavement in front of him. "You ungrateful fuck. Tell me your name! Tell me your fucking name!" Nothing, crickets in the night. He stood up and stomped on its head. "Why are you doing this to me?" Still nothing—boring stars, a light breeze.

He went back into his room and got his Zippo fluid from the Bible drawer. "This is it, you fucker," he said, dowsing it in fuel. "You don't start talking, you go up in flames. Got it? Tell me something, you sonofabitch." Still nothing. The sound of someone coughing in a distant room. A couple fucking in a nearby car. "Fine," he said, reaching down, crouching and flicking sparks with his lighter. "I don't like you." Within a second or two *flick flick* a load of light filled his face. He could feel the heat through the heat, the ashes rising and becoming one with the night. He stood there and waited until the plush alien was nearly only carbon embers, stomped it into the asphalt, and went back inside.

He went to bed smelling of fumes, tossed and turned all night, and woke up at two. He popped a handful of melatonin, slugged down half a pint of whiskey, and then tried to tire himself out with his fist. Nothing worked. He had to piss. In the bathroom, shaking off, he noticed the discarded tag he'd cut off earlier in the day. He picked it up. He sat on the toilet with his phone and the tag and Googled the serial number on the back. An image popped up, then another. Strange feelings consumed him as he scrolled the images of toys—they burned inside him, confused him. It was hard to feel any pain or sadness. He wasn't mourning. Of course his son was dead—he missed someone. He just wasn't sure if it was the son he'd had or the son he'd wanted.

INSTRUCTIONS FOR MOURNING

She had come in pieces two weeks earlier with no instructions. I had to send off for them and wait. After a month, I found her instructions in the mailbox. I put a stone at each corner of the paper to hold it still beneath the fan in our bedroom. The instructions were simple. I had her pieced together in less than an hour. But when I got up and stood her up so we could stand side by side together, she had a wobbly leg. I leaned her against the bed and tightened the bolt, got her back on her feet again, poised, perfect. And put her down, laid her down, and slipped her head on her pillow on our bed. Then I slid mine right beside it. Her bald head startled me. It made me think of my wife, back when she was sick, before and after she died. I found the black bag amongst the rubble of her packaging, pulled her hair from it. The little tube of glue was hidden at the bottom. I got the glue on her hair and her hair on her head. I decided to get some more light in the room so I could take her all in. I flipped on the lamps and opened the blinds. She almost gleamed, near shiny, just as I dreamed she would. We lived like this forever, or nearly so. Whatever forever we had.

I still have her other wigs in a box somewhere. I have not found the instructions to find them.

DOG PERSON

For over an hour she'd been thinking about killing the baby. Was it a baby? A toddler? He sprawled between two exhausted, resigned parents four rows behind her. They had been in the air for six hours, somewhere over the Pacific, and she'd just had it already with the carts of stale food, the fake smiles, the snoring old men, and now, now more than anything, the crying of the kid, especially after having had the worst sex of her life that morning. It went on and on and on. She tried to plug her ears with her fingers, some meditation, headphones—nothing canceled the sound. She could hear the blood in her head. Then the movement of her thoughts, the stars becoming nothing, dying—she could hear it all. Suddenly broken, she jolted up from her seat, and started over the man next to her. No doubt she was going to shut that stupid loud-mouthed lump of flesh up—break its neck, smother it with a pillow, maybe even flush it down the fucking toilet—*glug glug glug*. But then something happened. The last passengers, the inconsiderate few who still had their lamps on, cut the lights off almost simultaneously. It was kind of like a magic act. Maybe it was magic, period. And just like that, as the darkness moved in and consumed them, the kid finally shut up, didn't peep even a wheeze of air, as though the sound of his tears had been vacuumed clean out of him.

She sat back in the seat, slunk down, closed her eyes, and began thinking about how horrible she had been—thinking such thoughts. Then her brain started in on another thing she didn't want to think about. The lazy, half-assed, unprotected sex she'd had that morning in her hotel room in Mumbai. He was a sexy Welsh man, fifteen years her junior, named Albert. She'd been excited, after meeting him at a bar near her hotel. She was immediately charmed by him—his wit, his accent, his seeming decency. They'd spent the night together, had some fun, but he didn't know the first thing about pleasing a woman, clearly, could hardly even locate the clitoris, his tongue making motions in all the wrong directions. Something she just chocked up to inexperience.

When she finally started to doze the man sitting next to her woke up and decided he wanted to chat. Talked on and on and on about his business opportunities in China, Tech this and that, blah blah blah, on and on about how cool and young and rich he was—a monologue for the ages.

Finally, he said, The name's Jeff.

She shook his hand, didn't say anything.

Well, he said. What should I call you?

Jill, she said, unsmiling.

Jill, he said. What a pleasure. You get those eyes from Zales, because they sparkle like diamonds.

She laughed, rolled her eyes. Sure, she said. Something like that. Actually, I think it was Helzberg.

After a few seconds of awkwardness from Jeff, she said, Listen, man. That fucking baby's done crying and we have four hours left on this flight. I'd like to be asleep for all of them. Sorry. Nice to talk to you and all, but I'm going to sleep, if I can.

Jeff nodded, said, Understood. Get some rest.

She woke up upon landing at LAX. She ignored Jeff's small talk. When they got off the plane, he followed her—first to baggage claim, then to a vending machine. She hardly noticed him at first, yet there he was, tapping his foot, all smiles and waves outside the bathroom when she emerged, air-drying her hands, flapping them like weird wings.

Hey you, he said. I've been thinking. You like cats? I've got two at home. I'd love to take you out for a drink and show you my cats.

Ted, she said. I mean Ned. I mean Cody…

It's Jeff, he said.

Well, Jeff, you see…the thing is…

Come on, he said. One cat, couple drinks…

You're nice and all, she said. Thing is I'm a dog person. I wouldn't save a cat to save your life. Sorry bub, just not interested.

But, he said. But he didn't finish. She'd already turned away, had gained a few yards between them.

He watched as she faded into the crowd, her name in his head like an echo increasing in volume. By the time she hailed a cab, she couldn't recall his face—and she didn't like dogs, either. Her name wasn't even Jill. It was Amy.

The cab driver played reggae the whole ride home. It was the same and yet totally different from New York—more of a sprawl, a different smell. She'd only been in LA for six months, working as a showrunner for a popular Netflix series. She was a natural born writer, her stories occasionally appearing in the esteemed New Yorker. She told the cab driver her real name. He told her his. His name was Raheem. They small-talked over Bob Marley and the Wailers. She was truthful, except for her job. She said she was a veterinarian who specializes in cats.

I hate cats, he said.

She didn't say anything, just smiled big and wide, nodding.

How do you feel about screaming children on airplanes? she asked.

Can't stand them, he said. I'd do anything to shut the little shits up.

I wanted to murder the kid on my flight.

Maybe you should have, he said.

When he dropped her off, she threw her bags in the entryway of her apartment, kicked off her shoes and went into the kitchen. Fridge flung open, she chugged down half a Bud Light and let out a burp. She felt a little grimy so decided to shower. As the hot water fell over her body, she recalled the screams of the child on the plane. She slid her fingers up and down, up, down, all over her body, lathering.

When she got out, she saw she had a text from her girlfriend, Myra. It was a meme of the president saying something asinine, sporting an I-think-I-just-shit-my-pants face.

She texted Myra back: One day we'll drink from his fucking skull.

She entertained the idea of telling Myra about her trip, didn't feel the energy.

In her robe, she peeped through the blinds out into the courtyard and saw a young couple smoking cigarettes on a bench.

She remembered his name. His name was Raheem. He was the nice one. The screaming child in her head stopped screaming. It had nothing to do with him, though, nothing whatsoever. It was just a memory, a thought. But maybe it was something he said. She wasn't sure. Probably not. It was a little over the-morning-after, but she knew she'd be going to see her doctor soon. She didn't want anybody following her.

ORTHODONTICS

My buddy Ed and I had just left the beach and a guy wearing a dolphin shirt came out of the gas station on the corner swinging handcuffs like he was tricking with a yo-yo. He was taking swigs out of a bottle of Listerine. So he swung his handcuffs and swigged and swigged again and then he stopped cold in his tracks, slammed the bottle down into the concrete, and started talking all this shit about how the world is flat. That's when we noticed the cop. He was getting up off the ground near the entrance, dusting himself and wiping blood from his lips, yelling, "You stupid motherfucker, I'll shoot you." The dolphin shirt guy's eyes got real wide and he came running towards us, jumped right into the backseat of my car and said, "Let's roll." And that's exactly what we did. We peeled ass out of there, drove recklessly through the side streets, not even talking, just in a blind panic, and that's how we all ended up back at my place, sweating and anxious.

His name was Charlie and he said he'd been dodging cops all day. I offered him some water. He declined and requested something hot, so I put on some coffee.

I said, "Why're they after you?"

"Don't know. I think it's because they know my thoughts. They don't like what they see," he said.

Ed was cool as a frozen-ass cucumber. He just sat at the table reading the paper while his burrito cooked in the microwave. I wasn't so cool, though. I was pacing and asking questions and stuttering and tripping over myself. Finally, I found my weed and it made my heart tick a bit slower, a small laughter in my veins, but I was still a bit wigged out by the whole thing.

I looked at Ed. He shrugged.

"Seriously," I said. "What the fuck was I thinking? We don't even know him."

Charlie laughed. "Charles Baker," he said, "straight out of Kansas City, Missouri. Been here ten years and change. I punched that pig back there for harassing a kid buying a Snickers bar. Don't get me wrong, I'm plenty drunk, but that fucker had it coming either way you look at it—the smug fuck."

"I thought you said he didn't like what he saw inside your head," I said.

"That too, that too, but that fucker had it coming."

Ed chewed his burrito slowly, talked through his food. "I like you. Here, have a seat, man. Pigs are always up to some shit, aren't they?"

"You got that right," said Charlie, sitting down. "One of them stole my son and put a computer chip in his butt—and he comes back home after a year or two and doesn't even know who the fuck I am."

I was still feeling pretty weird about everything, but eased up soon enough, especially when Charlie got to talking about how the world is flat again. I knew it was stupid. Something about it, though, just closed off all the nerve points and made me numb. And after an hour or two, I really started to like him.

We played checkers and smoked weed while watching Jeopardy. And that Charlie, he was smart as a whip. One question was about a book by some guy named Boccacio. "What is the Decameron?" said Charlie. And the girl on the screen said the wrong thing, and old Alex Trebek said, "Oh, I'm sorry, Gina, the right answer is the Decameron. The Decameron." Ed and I just looked back and forth at each other unbelieving. Whole game went on like that.

During a commercial break Charlie asked if he could use the phone, so I threw him my cell. He dialed and let it ring and got no answer, tried again. Maybe it was a different number, I don't know, but this time somebody answered, and he said, "You got some? Yeah, okay. Well, long story. I guess you could probably just come over here. I got some new friends. Yeah, yeah, they're cool as fuck. Hey, hold on. Hold on." He motioned for me to come over. "Hey, could you talk to her? My friend Vicki, she needs directions."

I don't know why, but I gave her directions.

"That's right," I said. "No, no, a left, a left at the McDonalds."

I found her voice annoying, but was intrigued, and I thought maybe we could make it into a party, just the four of us.

She was there within the hour and we still had another episode of Jeopardy to go. But before she joined us, she opened her bag and pulled out a box of Cheerios, a compass, and a little baggy of meth, which Charlie proceeded to smoke out of what appeared to be a lightbulb.

"What's the compass for?" I asked.

"Getting around." She said.

Vicki beat Charlie by one question. He took it well. Ed and I lost by a ton so we decided to start in on the booze, get some music playing, and see how fast we could kill our loss-bummer and start smiling again.

We all did our best at taking in the chemicals around us quickly and then we sat around waxing philosophic. Charlie talked on and on about the great literature of the world. And Vicki kept going about the flatness of the earth.

"Bullshit the earth's flat," said Ed. "Where the fuck you people come up with this shit?"

"Well," she said. "Don't you see? The oceans and rivers would fall off into space if the world was round."

"Fuck no—it's called gravity," he said. "The fact that rivers flow and waves exist are fact enough it's a globe."

"I don't know," I said. "Let's hear Vicki out."

"Ain't shit else to hear," she said. "I already said it all."

"Okay," said Ed. "Explain this. If the world is flat, how come nobody has ever taken a picture of the edge?"

"Because it's far too big, no one could possibly make that journey."

"Bullshit," said Ed.

"Come on," I said. "I think she might have a point."

A few hours later, she cornered me in the bathroom while I was peeing, and said, "I'll show you my edge."

I said, "What about Charlie?"

"He's my brother," she said, but I knew she was lying.

We went at it for a bit, right there in the bathroom, then she left, just shy of a few strokes in, because I was feeling a little

28

woozy and she wanted to give me some space. But I'm telling you, it felt like real love somehow—something about the way she worked her mind and body.

When I woke up the sun was spiking me in the face with footballs. Ed was tied up in the kitchen. Charlie and Vicki were gone. Nothing seemed amiss until I untied Ed and said, "Fuck, what a night. Let's go surf."

"I'm down," he said.

But when we got out into the garage, we saw that those motherfuckers had stolen our surfboards right off the roof of my car and left all their bullshit behind. For instance, her teeth marks are still on my collarbone. That was weeks ago. She's already moved on, a new life in another land. I hope she comes back for her box of cereal, her compass, and her stupid denial that the world is somehow beautifully round and spinning, but I'm not holding my breath. Still, think of it, I could have promised her a future with braces and a glow-in-the-dark retainer so her teeth would never ever shift again. I could have given her walks to the beach on Sunday mornings with our make-believe child. I could have taken her to that impossible edge and pushed her off. Next time, if there ever is one, I think I'll loop a rope around her long front tooth and tether her here to this earth. She wouldn't need a compass. She wouldn't need anything. Charlie wouldn't have to exist. Neither would I. She could have it all.

BLOOD

Blood doesn't come out of a puncture much more than a dot. You could run a sharpened dowel through somebody and yank it out and you'd barely see a drop or two. I don't even know why they bother with the cotton swab after a shot. Just roll your sleeve down and move on. That's how my brother does it. Sometimes there might be a smear of bleed-through, but it's rare that you'll see it. Dark colored shirts, an expert. He doesn't bother rolling them down for me, though. He knows I know what he does. I don't care anymore, honestly. So we hang out and drink at my place most of the time, just trying our best to close out our past lives on a happy note. He sneaks off to the bathroom, shoots up his heroin on the toilet and nods there for a while—couldn't shit if he wanted to. Then he comes back and nods on the couch. I talk to myself and watch CNN. I finish off the rest of the beer and light a roach I've been eyeing in the ashtray, say, "Fuck, man. It's been so nice catching up these last few months, hasn't it? I'm so glad we put our differences behind us." I don't know who I'm talking to, the corpse on the couch or the roach in my hand. Either way, I'm happy to be present. I feel his pulse—faint. He's good. I roll him on his side so he won't choke on his puke or tongue or whatever. And he's still breathing, so that's good, too. But I have to shit and it might be a minute, so I set the alarm on my phone and put it right on top of his left ear, volume maxed— five minutes. And when I come out, it's a slight miracle—he's still there, still breathing, kind of opening his eyes and trying to talk directly into the wide mouth on the TV screen, the scream of the alarm drilling into his eardrum. I turn off the alarm, put him back into a sitting position and ask him, "You like this show?" I take his silence as a 'yes' and start looking for more booze, find a fifth I forgot I'd hidden from myself in an air vent near the kitchen. I drink about half of it down and think about how we got here as brothers. I was going over to his place for the first couple of weeks we started talking again. But that routine changed when I popped in one day and he was eating expired cottage cheese from the tub, the bottom of the spoon all burnt up with carbon. I started falling into my old ways of judging him and told him to come over and eat out of my fridge anytime he wanted. He pretty much lives here now. The couch is his and the bed is mine. He starts mumbling for a cigarette. I put one in his mouth and light it. He just lets it dangle, puffs once in a while, and stares into the TV screen, oblivious.

I wake up ten hours later and it smells like ammonia. A hand brushes my face and wipes at the carpet in front of me, does it again. My head feels filled with nails and my pants and shirt are wet. A whiff of puke and piss works its way through the cleaner. I sit up and my brother is throwing paper towels into the trashcan in the kitchen. I watch him as he leans over the counter and sniffs something up his nose. The entire apartment is clean. He's moving about quickly, with purpose. "How you feeling, brother?" he says. I rub my eyes and say, "I could use a beer." He cracks the fridge and throws me one, says, "Saw you were out so got some more." He snorts more stuff up his nose and says, "You have to try this shit." I say, "What is it?" He blinks, wipes the counter top down and says, "Meth. And I'm telling you, man, this is some high tier shit." I say, "Fuck it, maybe I'll give it a shot." He looks a little concerned, says, "Seriously? All I'm saying is—good shit." I chug down half of the beer. "Never done it," I say. "Never done much more than weed and coke." He rubs his chin, staring at me. "I'm telling you," he says, "I think it might be the first time in my life I felt alive."

Two hours later there's a needle in my arm. When my brother pulls it out, I imagine rivers of blood filling the floor at my feet. Also, I wonder what the spoon will look like when I start feeling like I'm hungry enough to eat.

THE FIGURATION OF MISS HOOK

I saw a woman with no arms, no legs, and no hair, he says, *barely even had a face*. She drinks in breaths of air, cools her fevered temples with a tepid rag, listening. *It was something*, he says. *She was at the gas station with a kid, maybe twelve years old, who was pulling her around on a little red wagon. He bought her cigarettes*, he says. *The clerk, I guess, didn't know what to do, so he sold this little kid a pack of cigarettes*. Laughter. *Speaking of which*, she says, and she makes a motion with her hand. He slides a fresh pack her way through the crumbs on the table. *Anyways*, he says, *you would've had to've been there*. She lights a cigarette and imagines the street below her. Twelve stories down. Traffic bends to the form of the river. There is snow quilted over the sand. She reaches over to touch his face, feels a waft of cold air, and wonders if he is still there beside her. *Please*, she says, closing her blind eyes to the darkness. *What do I look like?* She waits and waits. Then she gets her response in the form of violence. She bangs on the wall, tells her neighbors to keep it down or she'll call the cops. Then she laughs. *Let it rain*, she says. *Build a boat for the torso.*

CALCULUS

Calculus, 8:00 A.M.—Concentration is already an issue, even when I'm on my meds, and this asshole named Martin, who knows where I sit and why, was in my spot when I came running into class five minutes late. I took a seat in the back, deciding it was a waste to even try to pay attention. It was spite on his part, no doubt, a power play, him just being his dickhead self, probably because I'd fucked him within the first week of class then ghosted his ass, like, *man, I don't owe you shit, get it?* And like most men, he didn't get it, would refuse to get it, like, I just wanted to have some sex, no strings attached, that's all, and he's all wanting to tell me he's in love and stuff. I tried to explain to him that I've already been through middle school. He told me he felt used, and I told him, *So what? Did you enjoy yourself? That's what it's all about, not some gooey dating bullshit. You should be happy.*

After class, I told Martin to go fuck himself for taking my seat then went to meet up with Christina at the Student Center. I was starving, but had no money for food, so I drank lukewarm coffee from a Styrofoam cup while she talked on and on about her weekend in Boston, all the food she'd consumed, all the booze she'd drank. I hardly caught any of it, just heard blips of sound and nodded, occasionally said, *Damn, you serious?*

That was the only class I had on Tuesday, so when Christina finally ran out of breath, I went home and masturbated to an old X-Files episode until I was tired enough to go back to sleep. When I woke up, I had a text from this guy Kevin who I met at Club X one night last semester. Took him long enough—I think he was scared of me. It was either me or my penchant for trying to get some pegging done inside those strange wide folds of a sloppy night. I tried with him, as is my modus operandi, but, trust me, there's no convincing anybody when you're dealing with a nerd of that magnitude.

Chelsea called me around noon. "I'm pregnant. Again."

"Yeah, what's new?" I said.

"It's already grown quite a bit. I'm three months into this thing," she said. "I'll have to have a *real* abortion."

I knew what she meant by *real*. She ate morning-after pills like they were candy.

"I'm sorry, girl. Whose is it?"

"That guy Kevin. The guy you hooked up with last semester," she said.

"That's totally weird—he just texted me out of the blue, wants to take me out for some beers sometime."

"Really?!"

"Don't worry, I haven't responded yet."

"What're you going to say?"

"Obviously I'm going to tell him to get lost."

"No, for real, you should go," she said. "Seriously. He doesn't know I'm pregnant. You should go, for real. Get the inside scoop."

"I have no interest in doing that," I said. "He got super pissed when I suggested doing butt stuff. He yelled at me. Said, 'What, you think I'm a faggot?' and I was like, 'No, dude, it's just something people do, okay, chill.'"

"He said faggot?"

"I know, right? Total douchebag," I said.

"Probably has a tattoo of Elliot Rodger on his foreskin."

I laughed. "Yeah, we need to get ourselves a couple of Chads, don't we?"

"Yup, I'm tired of these incel assholes. I don't even want to ask him for money. He's probably one of these dudes who will try to tell me I have to keep it, you know."

"Oh, definitely, he shouldn't know about it," I said.

The alarm on my nightstand went off, signifying lunchtime with dad. We had lunch together twice a week, even though I couldn't stand him. It was just one way around not having to eat Ramen or Mac N Cheese for the umpteenth time in a day.

"Hey, Chels, I have to go. Lunch with dad. Call me later, okay? All right, love you. Talk soon. Bye."

We always ate at Applebee's. We always sat in a booth. My dad always ordered the same thing. I always tried something different. This time it was a monstrosity called a brunch burger—a cheeseburger with hash browns and a fried egg, loaded with ketchup. I scarfed it down while my dad told me he was thinking about leaving my mom. He kept talking and talking and I kept chewing and averting my eyes.

"Well," he said. "What do you think I should do?"

I burped and grabbed my stomach. "Goddamn, that was a lot of food."

He just looked at me, waiting, sipped a bit of his Coke.

"I'll tell you one thing—I'm going to have to abort this fat-ass food baby in a minute. Hope you're cool with that."

"Jesus Christ," he said, unamused. "Can't you take me seriously for even ten goddamn minutes?"

"What do you want me to say?" I said. "You want me to comfort you—tell you it is okay to leave my mother? You're fucked. Sure, that's what I say, dump the bitch. Is that what you want from me?"

He looked embarrassed, ashamed, and I was good with that, even though a part of me felt sorry I'd made a scene.

He drove me back to my apartment without uttering a single word. I stood in the parking lot for a minute, wondering what in the hell was wrong with me, I mean why couldn't I have just kept my mouth shut? But also, my mother didn't deserve to be deserted like that, did she?

I went into my bedroom and sprawled on my bed, watched General Hospital on mute while texting Kevin. I told him I was not interested in going out for drinks, not in the least, not ever, and he should just up and lose my number, because, frankly, *I'm way out of your league, dude.*

He never texted back, thank god.

Chelsea called me later that night, as promised, and said she wanted me to go to the clinic with her next Tuesday. I told her, "Of course. I'll be there. Hang in there. Try not to freak about it or anything."

"I'm feeling all right," she said. "Thanks for being so good to me."

"Of course—I love you, boo. I'll see you tomorrow"

I called my dad and canceled our lunches for the next couple of weeks. I said, "Sorry, dad, but I can't handle you anymore. I'm not your fucking marriage counselor. Maybe if you want to get together sometime and ask me how I'm doing, we can do that. But for now, until that can happen, I don't want to see you for a while."

I hung up the phone and a sad satisfaction rippled through me. I couldn't believe that this life we live is real, and all you can do is try to make the most of it, you know, even when everybody and everything is so fucked up, including yourself.

I had to vent, so called Christina, told her all about my shitty day, and that golden bitch, she let me.

"Wait," she said. "Maybe your mom should peg your dad."

"No. Gross."

"Seriously," she said.

"Fuck off. No."

"I mean, you never know," she said. "Maybe then he'd see the light."

HOOKS

A few days after I heard the news, that he'd tried to carve a hole for himself inside the earth, I wondered if it were possible for a man to rip out his own vocal chords. One night, I actually Googled it, came up with a bunch of misleads. Wouldn't have mattered anyway—I'd just get a little black board and hang it around my neck and write it all down for him with chalk. The things I saw, the thoughts I had. Voices still exist, even if you can't hear them. Maybe it all came down to selfishness. For a minute I thought I'd just swallow down some fish hooks and rip them back out of me and hope for the best—what I'd call "trying to be a good friend."

Often he'd stand at the corner outside Al's, sipping at his Mocha while holding court with himself, just talking and blabbing away to nobody. If anybody tried to join him, which, as friendly and welcoming as his smile was, was often, he'd clam up and do more drinking than talking, staring right though their caring faces out beyond and over the dirt road to a place where the sun patched the hills with gold.

He hadn't always been like that, sure, that all started up after Marti took the Mazda and hitched a U-Haul to the back, stuffed all of her belongings into it, and headed off into the great belly of America, telling him she had to go out and find herself, where exactly she fit in in this too-short disaster called life. That's when he stopped talking, around then, even though he kind of still talked to me. You couldn't call it conversation, or exposition, or anything, really, other than short observational bursts, guarded clues into the state of his thinking. I even made him go to the doctor one time, and not without a fight, either, because I figured maybe he'd had a miniature stroke or something, but Dr. Bruner said he was healthy. His face didn't droop any more than usual and he still seemed to walk just fine.

After the attempt, though, he had to spend a few weeks locked away with some head doctors out in Mulridge County. The day he got out, I went over and found him in his rocking chair on the front porch whittling away at some totem he held tightly in his palm. From where I stood, it looked like he'd fashioned himself a tiny baby.

"Hey, Scott," I said. "Long time no see."

He looked up and nodded, kept whittling away at the infant, sweat beaded along his brow in thin rows. I detected in the dying light a few streaks of gray in his sideburns. He was only twenty-five and starting to age at a rapid clip, though his face remained boyish, in fact, strangely so, and you couldn't help but think that there were a million other faces that were just the same, you'd just never seen one.

He finally folded and pocketed the knife, set the baby on a

little table to his left, and said, "Finn. Been a minute."

"What'd you carve there?" I said.

"Marti," he said.

"Looks like a baby."

"It's Marti," he said.

"All right, then," I said. "Marti it is. How're you feeling?"

He didn't say anything, just nodded.

"Looking good," I said.

He lit a cigarette, took a long pull and sighed, staring off through the lighted windows of the house across the street.

"Well," I said. "I'll go ahead and get out of your hair. Just wanted to stop by and say hi, that's all. Don't want to be a bother."

As I was walking away, I heard him.

"Sure is hot," he said.

I turned around. "Hit ninety-seven today," I said.

"Hot," he said.

I nodded right into an immense moment of silence and just kept nodding.

"Want to come in?"

Still nodding, I followed him in and sat at the dining room table, a darkly varnished thing littered about with unopened mail, while he rummaged through the fridge.

"Want a Coke or something?"

"That'd be great," I said.

He sat down across from me, offered me a cigarette.

"Thanks," I said, but he just sat there staring at me, not saying a word.

We smoked in silence for a while, sipping our Cokes.

"I have to clear the air," he said.

"You don't have to do that, trust me. It's okay. Don't worry about it."

"It's not Marti. It's my job. My job's got me all fucked-up," he said.

"You're an IT guy, right?"

He nodded. "You don't know the half of it."

"The half of what?" I said.

"My job."

"Well?"

"I work in the city." he said.

"And?"

"I sit at a table with rows of other people. These people, they do the exact same thing as me."

"Yeah?"

"I worry about them." he said. "They don't even know what kind of damage they're doing to themselves."

"What do you mean?"

"What I do. You want to know what I do?" he said.

"Of course."

"All the evil shit you hear about being online. My job is to view all that shit and decide whether or not it should be scrubbed from the internet."

"Seems like the lord's work to me," I said. "Why you feel so bad about it? Somebody has to do it. It's honorable, right?"

"You just don't get it. Nobody gets it. Marti didn't get it. You don't get it. The doctors don't get."

"Hey, hey, slow down," I said. "I'm sorry. I didn't mean to upset you."

"I'm not upset. Just get on, you should go. But, come on, man, finish your Coke first. Don't want it going to waste."

I chugged the Coke down and said, "You need to chill, man. Calm down. I love you."

"There's no such thing," he said.

"Whatever, man," I said. "I'm leaving."

When I got out onto the porch I took his stupid little wooden baby he'd carved and threw it across the street into the neighbor's yard. My anger got the best of me. I started thinking about how if he tried killing himself again, he'd do well to pick out a surer method. Rather have him dead than crazy.

We didn't talk much after that. His hair grew long. He stopped going to Al's, recused himself from the world around him. And in a way, so did I.

Maybe if I could've kept my mouth shut long enough, his silences would've been voice enough for me to "get it." Perhaps that's the real matter, after all—"getting it."

It's never so much the swallowing that hurts, it's the ripping out. If fish hooks could talk, I swear to god they'd tell you to run.

PREACHER WITH FRUIT

The preacher pulls back on his hangnail in the dark, cuts. A mosquito sucks from a slender vein in his old saggy neck. He lifts a dry hand to the dark air, rethinks, and settles it back against his pant leg, smooths away at wrinkles there.

A barbeque smell to the air: fires and canned beans. The preacher comes out from the tent, sits on a chair in front of a small fire. There is a dented bucket beside him calloused over with rust. He retrieves a handful of mulberries from it, pops them in his mouth, chews them slowly. His hands and mouth look bruised, turning more deeply red, almost black, with each swallow. He washes his hands with a bottle of water, dries them on his pants then claps them together.

A mother brings her child to the preacher's tent because the preacher is the only one there with a blade. The boy is shallow-breathed and dry about the lips. His tongue, folded, sticks to the backs of his teeth. The preacher sets the kid down on a little stool in front of him. He blesses him, then begins slashing at the boy's hair.

The preacher tugs some strands and indiscriminately strokes the razor through. A shock of hair the size of a cigarette box falls to the ground. It covers an anthill. The boy looks down. The ants have begun gathering bits and pieces of the boy's hair and taking off with them.

The child watches the ants. He knows he should talk with the preacher instead of just sitting, but he has lost his words.

There. Now that the hair's gone, says the preacher, let's get you all the way cleaned up.

The child looks pleadingly at his mother, hoping she sees. She smiles and nods and lets the preacher proceed. As the preacher begins carving into his scalp, the child prays and watches the ants drown in his urine.

POST-APOCALYPTIC BOYHOOD
WITH PARAMEDIC

In the afternoons, the younger children play in an open field across the street from the camp. Wooden planks wind-torn from homes have been transformed into forts and castles and racecars. Tree limbs are gripped in armpits and pulled eye-level, accumulating as silent guns. They've transformed pinecones and acorns into hand grenades by attaching small twigs at the tops that they pull out with their teeth.

The sky seems riddled with the brightest incandescence at night, like bullet holes through a black wall, letting millions of pinpoints of seepage through, the seepage of another world, like tiny question marks smudged against bleak tapestry.

A few of the boys, out late and unattended, point their sticks upward towards the stars and make the noises they've only ever heard in movies and video games, searching after each burst for any sign of new light.

And it can be seen there, in the dark, it is there, engraved in their postures before the vast expanse of pasture, that they actually have only begun to pretend and wonder at the things beyond the tatters in the sky.

The kids in the pasture, Paramedic watches them from a quiet distance tonight. It's impossible to know another man's thoughts; but he's thinking, not exactly this but something similar to this: *I wish I were young again. I wish I were young and naïve and stupid. I wish I could still make-believe in real heroes like these fools do. I wish I could kill them all and feel something bad deep within me.*

He takes his notebook from his back pocket and scribbles in the dark.

From paramedic's notebook: September 23rd 2011:

I reckon I miss you mom. Reckon. What a word. Reckon. Recon. Reckon.

I reckon I miss her. I miss her hair, that strawberry fire of hair, that ugly tangle.

Her head looked especially terrible with the new dye job and curls, the perm, the whatever, that cost sixty bucks plus the ten-dollar tip she slipped Angela, on the way out. Dad was there when she got home, drinking a six and watching the game, and he told her what he thought, what indeed we all thought about the new fiery swirls. Sissy laughed, moving a toy car across the linoleum in the kitchen. George told Sissy to "be a quiet little angel for mama", and, pivoting on the heel of his left foot, told mom that her horrible new red hair looked really quite nice on her. His words made her feel young and attractive and worthy of husband for a moment, and you could see this, in the eyes, under the artificial lights. She said, "Thank you, Georgie. Thank you. I just knew somebody'd love it." Leave it to George, the nice guy, to shovel out such lies, to hide behind that fickle mask of his. I just sat there with dad, staring, not knowing what to say, or whose side to take, and besides, I was sucked into the vacuumed silence of a cough syrup-induced coma-like state, so, you know, what could I do but listen? Do I have to play the hero every time he drinks beyond limit and gets lippy with mom? If it came to fists, I'd step in, sure, per the usual smoke signals on a Saturday night. But it didn't come to that, not this time, and I felt grateful to the ceiling fan for that, among all the other things above. Uncle Steve was over eating on some pork rinds and puffing like a chimney on his Marlboros, and when I felt the good elixir had tired of its course through my veins, I went in to see about some beer and pretzels. Solitaire was sprawled before him, awash in ash, sticky, unlucky, and he just sitting with a trucker's grin, big and bare, staring down, searching for royalty. I patted his back into buckling with fright. "How's the game?" I took a seat beside him, popped a fresh beer, and sifted through the butts in the ashtray for a long one. "Nothing can fool me, boy," he finally said. Smoke swam out through the reeds of his teeth, up across the 60 Watt bulbs above, washed over the ceiling, and disappeared into the pores of the house. "Well, looks to me like that table sure did." "Hell you say, boy! Obviously you don't know your very own uncle very well. Watch this," he said, self-assured and with a dangerous look in his eye. "I take this guy and put him over here. Then this guy comes over here. You see...progress. Then this guy..." He paused quite a longish while, tapping his fingers against his skull. "Then...well, fuck...I think it's over, boy," he said. "Ain't that some shit, outsmarted myself again, and you, you think it's too easy. Shit..." "You're still a good dude, regardless. Even if you *are a shitty card player, at least you have that," I said, a jackal of a smirk pinned to my teeth. "Shit…" he said, "did you see what your mother did to her hair? Goddamn awful, looks something dreamt in nightmares and spit out into the world as a warning." I shrugged and went to bed. In the morning I found that dad had slept on the couch all night. Mom was already gone to wherever she had gone, only later I found out where. She'd been back trying to get a refund for the dye job, begging Angela to get it back to a similar state to what it had been before. She cried when she came home, still a red head; apparently Angela wouldn't do another job for free. Nothing could be done; we didn't have that kind of money. That's when I told her, Just remember, momma, change is good, except when it's bad, and in this case, it's awful, and she cried harder and hid herself in her bedroom for three days. When she emerged, I apologized. She accepted it, told me she loved me; we hugged, a kiss on the cheek. And time went by as it does; a phantom, never changing; but her hair, her hair never looked the same again.*

THE POSTPONED SUN

It was a Tuesday, when my brother called to tell me he was, after half a life of substance abuse, finally sober. "Five months clean," he said. A portrait of his six-year-old self my father kept on his nightstand bloomed, curly-headed and pale, in my memory, lending some hope. But like all good things, within one breathless sentence, all hope vanished, just like that, and I heard myself saying, "Too soon to be asking for money." Silent disappointment was felt through the shared workings of our DNA. "You know, I'm getting my shit together," his blood said inside mine. "I know," stirred mine—and then my mouth started to move.

"Glad things are looking up, man."

He said, "Me too," and sighed.

"I love you," I said.

We hung up our ends.

A few months before, he'd nodded off at our father's funeral, then after, while I was holding a little urn, my brother said, "You'll have to give me a spoonful of pops. I want to mix him with some ink and get a tattoo."

Rachael, my wife, looked over in disbelief, laughing, only able to muster, "Really, John?"

I walked into the parking lot of the church, rage rippling my tongue. Out there, I smoked amongst Mormons and veterans and family, all of them there to memorialize a man they'd hardly ever known, same as me. Turns out you only get around to knowing folks when they're gone—when it's too late, as they say. But maybe too late is exactly the distance you need to feel some closeness, some love.

My aunt and uncle were there. We all stayed with my mother. It was weird not having my dad around. But the things I learned from those two, it made things easier. I hadn't seen them in years. Seems like estrangement is a common clause in our network—so is trauma. And so is fetishizing that trauma. Everything about my father made more sense through those two, his brother and sister, his blood, and it all worked itself slowly into me out there in the desert.

I could stare at the lizards on the fence for hours, wondering if they reminded my father of jungle lizards (there are such things, aren't there?), and if their presence brought back terrible memories of Vietnam, or if it all was so caged inside him, those feelings, he didn't know what or how to feel, if feel anything at all—and how stupid it all is, how it didn't matter anymore because he was dead and would never have to live it again, anyway.

I'm often reminded of ghosts because I'm named after one—my mother's cousin, a drowned three-year-old from the nineteen-fifties. Sometimes his body floats above mine when I sleep. It doesn't comfort me, but my mother says I shouldn't be afraid. And I'm not, I'm only reminded. There is a void that awaits all life on earth, both now and when, and knowing that never finds me any sleep, when sleep sometimes seems like the only comfort left behind.

On the airplane, coming back to Kansas, I dreamt of needles and mountain tops, the intersection of external beauty and internal feeling, the deceit that is sworn to you at birth, rendering your thoughts incompatible regarding your blood and who shares it.

In another dream, I threw up maggots. Eventually they grew into people, became my friends, my lovers—and then all was a ghost above me, a ceiling, blank, white, and my eyelids closed suddenly onto nothingness, and it was briefly beautiful to be alive.

SOMEDAY SOON

The alien invasion that wakes me up turns out to be an ambulance screaming down 1st Street, hauling Mrs. Crenshaw to god only knows what hospital or hell. Briefly, I feel evil thinking about the back rent she owes, but the stubbed toe takes care of that, head held high after the pain allays.

The duplex where we share a wall with Crenshaw still smells of yesterday's burnt toast. I scratch as I run the faucet in the kitchen a minute to get to the cold water going, a weird lump in my armpit. I briefly think about changing my deodorant brand, maybe I developed an allergy to it or something. I take some antihistamine and swallow from the faucet. The water isn't cold. I try to go back to sleep. It's useless, can't stop thinking. And to make matters worse, my cat is sprawled like road-kill across the sofa, sawing logs like a gaggle of asthmatic old farts.

It's only been a month since Roscoe left for Lisbon, commissioned to paint a mural on a large outcropping of rocks off the Atlantic coast, and I haven't slept well since he's gone, mostly due to my new schedule of trying to be awake enough to talk on the phone from different time zones. I started drinking coffee at night. Now I don't need the coffee, just can't sleep. When I do sleep, I have strange dreams, mostly of alien invasions and Dobermans ravaging my lifeless body over the rocks of some non-existent quarry. If I'm lucky, I catch an hour here and there before the dreams come. The ambulance that hauled Mrs. Crenshaw away wasn't a dream, just another reason to be awake, and Roscoe hasn't called in a week, so I'm awake all the time.

I spend the rest of the night and most of the day staring at the wallpaper, which is beginning to curl like ferns at the seams, while infomercials drone in my ears. I edge for an hour, watching the TV screen, a new record, and need some fresh air. Mrs. Crenshaw's dog, a little Pomeranian named Leo, greets me at the door. He seems hot, his tongue clenched out the side of his face, dangling. I get the mail and let him in, fill a bowl with water. From my place on the sofa, as I watch him drink in his scruffy reflection, I wonder if Mrs. Crenshaw has finally bitten the dust. Again, I think about the money she owes.

A few hours later, the phone rings. I dig it out of my pocket, hoping it is Roscoe, but it's a local number, so I ignore it. The same person calls me over and over and over again. Finally, I answer and say, "Leave me the fuck alone, please."

"Is that the way you talk to your tenants now?"

"I'm sorry, Mrs. Crenshaw. It's been a rough day," I say. "How are you? You okay? I saw the ambulance."

"I'm fine, just some palpitations. I'll be home in a jiffy," she says. "Actually, I wanted to talk to you about Roscoe."

Silence swells the signal like water rushing a hose.

"Well," I say. "What about him?"

"You know what?" she says.

"Huh?"

"I still have the knife that killed my brother," she says.

"What?"

"Now…what was it I was going to tell you? Oh yeah…"

"Where are you?" I say. "Are you with anybody? Hand the phone to somebody."

"Yep," she says. "I still have it."

The connection dies.

I call back numerous times over the course of several hours only to be greeted with a recording that says the number I am trying to reach is out of service.

It turns out tuna straight out of the can isn't so bad with a little salt on it. I sit on the sofa, dialing Roscoe, sprinkling my fish. When it goes to voicemail, I scoop some tuna into my mouth and try again. It's four in the morning, little Leo curled at my feet, the living room a cube of drab light. Pretending like you're living in the lap of luxury—what a joke. But I am pretending. The tuna I'm eating is caviar and my boyfriend hasn't left me for a young Portuguese boy. I make-believe things are fine and normal. *Soon enough I'll have enough money for the Nissan I've been eyeing*, I think. Then, I say it aloud.

The phone rings, waking me from some form of half-sleep at five-thirty in the morning, and Mrs. Crenshaw blurts before I can say anything, "I still have the knife that killed my brother."

"What are you talking about, Mrs. Crenshaw? Are you with somebody, anybody at all? Listen to me. Find somebody. Find somebody and hand them the phone, please."

"I need to tell you about Roscoe," she says.

"What the fuck is this, some kind of sick, geriatric joke? Just hand somebody the phone, Mrs. Crenshaw."

"Is that any way to talk to your tenants?" she says. "You know, I have to tell you something about Roscoe. I've had my suspicions for a long time now. Now, I don't know exactly how to say this, but I think he might be one of those, what do they call them, oh yes—a Sodomite."

"Are you serious?" I say, laughing. "He's my boyfriend. So yeah, definitely, we fuck each other—and I don't think I need to tell you about the entry-point, either."

"Oh, I don't mind that, I just thought you should know," she says. "And by the way..."

"What is it now?" I say.

"I still have the knife that killed my brother."

"What is it with you? You're really starting to creep me out."

"You'll see," she says.

"What the fuck is that supposed to mean?" I say.

A long period of breathing silence ensues, then knocking.

"Wait, wait, hold on, somebody's at the door."

I open the door, blinded by dawn, and seated on her rocking chair, just like always, Mrs. Crenshaw says, "Well, what a surprise? I haven't seen you in weeks."

"You're telling me. When'd they let you out? And what's with all these creepy phone calls about a knife and your dead brother?"

"What? What do you mean? What are you talking about?" she says.

"When did you get out of the hospital?"

"I don't know what you're talking about," she says. "Are you okay? You don't look so good."

She hoists herself to her feet.

"Here," she says. "Have a seat."

Dazed, I ignore her offer, spin right around and go back inside. Roaches scatter about within crevices in the walls as my phone rings. I reach into my left pocket, then the other, come up empty-handed, and realize the ringing is distant and muffled, leading me on a weird scavenger hunt into the kitchen, where I find it on top of the refrigerator in a box of Frosted Flakes.

"My god, you answered! I've been so worried about you!" says Roscoe.

"Me?" I say. "I thought you up and left me."

"I've been calling you all week. I almost called in a welfare check. I started thinking you were dead," he says.

"No…just…I lost my phone."

We talk awhile before my phone dies, maybe for good, and I start my search for the spade we bought for the garden we hadn't yet started.

I thought killing the cat was a dream I'd wake up from, but even still, it's a beautiful day, can't deny it. And the sun, that spun-gold heat beating into me as I dig, blooms into some kind of strange revelation of better things to come. I forget the stench of her mottled fur as I dig deeper and deeper into the earth, so effusive to the task I hardly notice the little dog licking at my feet. And so what about the rent? One day. Someday soon, perhaps.

DAYDREAM NATION

Hours were spent walking lengths of highway wagging my thumbs at passing cars. The sky overcast, ready to rain or hail. I didn't even have an umbrella, just shitty clothes that hadn't been washed in a decade. Fifteen miles, face gone red with sweat, burning, a tattooist named Gabriel picked me up. Just outside El Dorado. It was beginning to rain.

Gabe chain-smoked Pall Mall Lights and listened to hair metal, drumming his hands on the steering wheel and dashboard as he drove. He seemed to drive without any other purpose than that of occasionally swerving to hit dead animals and lisping Twisted Sister lyrics into the cab.

Fifty miles down, I was dry and happy and didn't mind the shitty music, the hand-drumming, or even the grotesque, calculated treatment of road kill. I just wanted to be home, on my own soil. I wanted to lounge around on my old furniture, loiter inside my ex-wife, and fish the silver water next to Skillet rock, remember what it was like to be a boy discovering the world for the first time. And then Gabriel started telling me about his charms, his ability to read auras and palms, look into the depths of souls and tell people their futures. And I was bored, so I said, Shoot, tell me mine. And this plagiarist, he had the gall to tell me: *The weather will continue bad. There will be more calamities, more death, more despair. Not the slightest indication of a change anywhere. The cancer of time is eating you away. Your heroes have killed themselves, or are killing themselves. The hero, then, is not Time, but Timelessness. You must get in step...*

I left him with his neck like a rubber band on the shoulder of the highway, because, as it turns out, I'd learned to read while I was locked up, and there's nothing in this world I can't stand more than a fraudulent little fuck like him.

That's life, turns out.

I never knew what it was all about, why people do these things, but I'm telling you, what I'm about to tell you is, the sound it made when his neck snapped, it's the closest I've come to touching the spiritual, like dancing around inside the skins of ghosts. Only thing I regret is he didn't look the part of a politician.

WHAT WOULD YOU DO?

Janice rested the heel of her left foot on the edge of the bed, cotton balls wedged between her toes, and painted her nails. Martin had a collection of moths pinned beneath glass in a frame above his desk. He tapped the glass, inspecting them one by one and row by row, while throat singing; he hadn't had a lesson in years, not since graduating law school and passing the bar, but he still had it—sounded like an ancient monk hidden away in the Tibetan mountains, vibrating prayers deep into the rocks and snow. Janice fell back on the bed and let the paint dry beneath the ceiling fan, watching Martin as he executed his strange routine near the desk.

When he finished making noises, she said, "Aren't you going to fuck me? We haven't had sex in months."

"Oh, well, yeah," he said. "Did you forget you married an idiot?"

He slowly undressed. She watched him, letting her bathrobe fall open. They started slowly and mimicked each breath from the other. When they were done, Janice slumped down with all her weight on his body, cotton balls scattered about, and stayed there.

"What if I told you I killed somebody?" Martin blurted.

Janice laughed and rolled off him, sweat beaded over her body, glistening.

"No," he said. "Seriously, what if I told you I killed somebody? A child? What would you do?"

She hummed about the room, dressing into pajama bottoms, a torn t-shirt, and said, "What do you think I'd do?

"I don't know," he said. "You tell me."

"Well," she said. "I'd probably start calling you Lenny, tell you about the rabbits, get an abortion, and then tell you to go fuck yourself—something like that, maybe in a different order."

"Wait," he said. "Abortion?"

Janice left the room without explanation.

Martin stayed, staring at the ceiling, wishing he hadn't said anything.

A little later, Janice walked by the bedroom, said, "I'm going to watch some TV," and turned off the light. Martin fell asleep, laughing in the darkness she'd left him in, the glow from the hall slightly illuminating his bare chest as he breathed.

A THOUGHT AT INAUGURATION

I couldn't hear him breathe, that's how I knew. I pulled out my phone and pushed the 9. That's it, that's as far as I got. I hovered over his gaping mouth, waiting for something, anything, and then it started to rain. At that moment, I was looking at a stone, a wet stone. It took me a few moments to register him for who he was. Such must be the case after the soul evacuates the body. Smells like shit and looks like nothing. But he had a name. That's the difference. I renamed him then and there. Loser. Into the earth he would dissolve, become another layer of something, indistinguishable but there, and God, whatever that is, would abate with symmetry in dirt. And that would be the whole of the story. History would paint a still-life, I thought. And it will burn.

URBAN LEGEND

You've all heard the urban legend about the kids who went to drink some beers at an abandoned farmhouse on Halloween night, found a body hanging from the ceiling fan in one of the bedrooms, and, while running out the front door in utter shock, was confronted by a large man who hacked two of them to death with a machete, while the other two, securing their leaking blood with what pressure they could muster, ran two miles to safety?

It is no mere urban legend, I'll tell you that. Why else you reckon I have this plastic hand? You think this thing is fashionable?

Perhaps the myth is that there were any survivors at all. The word survivor is the lie and the legend.

Fuck it. Hand me a beer. Other hand, dipshit.

VISIONS OF THE NIGHTLIFE

For a while they called him Bomb-Toothed Bob. He'd gotten the nickname right off the plane from Afghanistan. After spending two months in a German hospital, he'd lost most of the lisp, when he actually started talking again. Lucky to be alive, that Bob—took shrapnel from a roadside bomb to the mouth, making tooth-sized tunnels straight through the back of his neck—tiny bone bullets the size of splintered wood. Knocked-out cold and mouth-shattered, he heard some Ja Rule song ring through his brain as he came to, tweety-birded stars haloing his head in his concussed delusion. For a long time now, it went like this: he would get better, healed, get out for a bit, go home, and then infection would start back in, repeat. Like now, he was back in the VA in Virginia, infections from his injuries having reemerged nearly overnight. He'd been there a week already, should've been out by now, but the nurse had just come by to tell him he'd have at least one more week of antibiotics, steroids, and rest to abide.

"Hey, Bob, you see the white light?"

It was Randy, the guy he shared the room with.

"Nah, nothing like that," said Bob.

"That's good. I saw it. It was like a white bulb burning brighter than the sun. Seemed pleasant enough, but I wasn't ready—seemed too hot for my blood," said Randy.

Randy was missing his right leg, still had a long recovery ahead of him. He'd been in there fighting off gangrene for months.

"It's a strange thing when you puke because you can't stand the smell of your own rotten skin," said Randy.

"Tell me about it," said Bob. "I have to taste it."

They fell silent, took naps between quips, shitty daytime television a soft glaze over the seeming quiet, that or they stared at their phones and complained about humanity—how lazy and stupid everybody seemed to be these days, referencing Facebook statuses and Twitter feeds. Neither one of them had family close enough to visit, so it was mostly just the two of them and the nurses all day and night. At least Bob could get up out of bed and walk around, he had that luxury. He just had to take the IV baggy with him, if he were getting his meds. Sometimes he'd sneak outside and look for cigarette butts worth smoking. And when he'd come back in smelling of smoke, the nurses lectured him—all the infection in his mouth and over the back of his neck, not to mention all the tar and death in his lungs.

"Fuck it, I smoke," Bob told them. "Not like I killed anybody."

He was only twenty-four years old, now and forever sporting a face filled with scars. Randy was twenty-six. He would be relearning how to walk here pretty soon. Bob didn't know who had it worse. And neither did Randy. They both imagined at certain times what it would be like trading places. But it always seemed as though they liked their own lives just fine—fine enough to live with, anyway.

Sometimes Bob would sneak Randy out and zigzag his wheelchair through the streets at dawn. He'd haul him three miles to the nearest liquor store, where they'd tie one on in the cratered parking lot and shoot the shit. And what a sight they were—twin IV baggies affixed to the left handle of the wheelchair, tubes like crazy straws going up and into their veins—sharing swigs from a fifth, crushed empty beer cans littered about wheels and feet. The manager of the liquor store, a redneck named Larry who called himself a patriot as often as he chanced a sentence or two, just let them do their thing, seeing as they were deformed veterans just wanting a little space and time that they could call their own.

They'd done this a few times now, joking about the things of life, but this time Bob's tone changed as a Hummer drove by and he unlocked something inside himself and it hurled itself out into the water-logged air.

"He put his gun under my chin," he said. "He told me 'this is how we get you grunts wet behind the ears, got it? It's either you or it's him. Now what's it gonna be?' That's when I saw who he was pointing at. It was a teenager, maybe fourteen, fifteen years old, carrying a jug of water about twenty-five yards to the north of us. I didn't want to, I knew it was wrong, but I just shoved his gun out from under my chin, took aim, and fired, fired maybe three or four times—stopped when he hit the ground. He was just as shocked as I was, surely. I still can't believe I did that. Same guy that made me do that died in the explosion that took my face. And you know what, can I tell you something? Sometimes, when I think to pray, I think of that day and pray the infection inside me gets me when I'm sleeping."

"I'm sorry, man" said Randy. "You hear these stories from time to time. I've always written them off as pure hoax, but you, I believe you. You're a good friend. You wouldn't fib about something like that. Some people are just plain animals. I served with a few of them. Thankfully, they're few and far between. Still, it's hard to watch a man kill with such glee in his heart, enemy or not. I had a few of them with me over there, would piss on the corpses, take pictures with them and stuff. I never did that kind of shit, though. Hell no. It's repulsive."

"Fix the body first, then the mind. That's what I've been thinking. I need to talk to somebody about it. I'm having nightmares again, wake up some nights to the smell of my face burning off and dead kids dancing through my head."

"That why you've been talking to yourself and tossing and turning lately?" asked Randy.

"Well, that and the heat—can't get comfortable."

"I'll ask Anita if she can bring us a fan," said Randy.

There was a bloated silence, pregnant, and then Bob said, "Randy? What I told you. Can you keep it between us? You're the only person I ever told."

Randy nodded, kept nodding for a minute, then said, "I suppose we better be heading back."

They successfully snuck in undetected and went to bed, wrapped up in each other's thoughts, a thin gauze of light from the TV screen, a cold glow about their sleeping faces.

In the morning Randy woke up to Anita, one of the nurses, lecturing Bob about sneaking off at night. "Be cool," he said. "We just needed something to do, that's all."

"I don't know how either one of you ever expect to recover, if you're always going off and getting drunk," she said. "You aren't even supposed to be moving around. You two have really bad infections. Do you even think?"

"Worst that could happen to a person has already happened to us," said Bob. "I'm not too worried about it. And you shouldn't be, either."

"Not like we killed someone," piped Randy. "We just had some beers. That's all."

Anita shook her head, putting the new IVs up to dangle like bats from those strange metal frames, then inserted tubes into their arms, but she refrained from looking them in the face.

"Say, Anita," said Randy. "You think you could find us a fan? It's blazing hot in here. Air's made of lava or something."

She looked at him, a mean stare, and walked out without a word, closing the door hard behind her.

They stayed put the next few days. Anita eventually brought in a fan. It was hard to hear each other over the drone. They stopped speaking to each other—watched the TV on mute, silently hoping the voices in the hallway would someday lend them a narrative.

SPEED DATE IN THE ER

It took me years of searching—endless socials, mixers, and awkward online chats—to discover that this is the only place to find the good ones, the ones who still feel something, no matter how damaged or uncertain their *feelings* may be.

Like this one, he's such a good-looking guy, but he keeps saying *fuck*, grabbing his junk, and rocking back and forth in his chair like an epileptic dog. Occasionally he catches me staring at him and tries to play it cool, hands back at his sides, smile on his face, but within a minute or two, he's back at it, grabbing his piece, rocking, and saying *fuck* loud enough for reception to hear it. When he finally looks up at me, he smiles, and I smile back, brushing the hair from my eyes. His face is filled with pain, but his eyes are honest, and his snaggletooth smile seems to be telling me *you can put your trust in me. I can learn to love you.*

He is moaning now, the word *fuck* no longer sufficient for conveying the slurred-feel of his pain, but he's still smiling occasionally, when our eyes run parallel a second and meet in the center, under these bright and sterile lights. I'll bet you he's reading my thoughts right now, seeing as I haven't worn that bonnet going on something like eighteen years. And I hope he is, too, and reading me deep and sideways, up and down, because then he'd know his worth in this world. Maybe he already knows it—that in this moment, right this second, he is the most important person in my life.

I wink, licking my lips, first the top one, then the bottom. I want to make him tremble inside of me. I want him to know that he is the chosen one, *the* one, and if he were capable of leaving his selfish pain long enough to read the twisted Braille of my brain, then he would be ball deep in pussy right now, but he only winces and clutches himself harder, closing his eyes to me, smile all gone and faded from his handsome face, limp and imperious, because he's deep inside himself, searching to find a compartment to store his grace.

The seventy-year-old next to him is staring at me. I squint to conjure the image of my father from him, blurred but spitting just the same, when a name is called, breaking my concentration, and the old man leaves the room right as I get the gumption to spread my legs for him.

If even for an instant I made him feel something deeper, if he'd gotten to the point of seeing inside of me, past his pain, then he would have never stopped looking.

And then a nurse comes up to me, holding a clipboard, and says, *Have you filled out your forms?*

No, I say, and I stand to leave. *I haven't. I'm not sick.*

Oh, she says. *Are you waiting for someone?*

I'm not sick, I tell her, but this time I say it in a hardened voice, pushing past her and through the crowd.

I walk away from the nurses, away from my anonymous and injured lovers, away from Darius and his mop, his bucket of suds, his brown clothes and janitor's nametag, hiding my smile behind my hands, but before I even make it to the EXIT sign, I drop my hands to my sides, retreating, and turn around.

Back in the thick of these hurt others, I yell at them to *come inside*, all of them, inviting them into my body as I open my mouth as wide as it will go. *Salvation*, I tell them, *salvation*. And before I know it, one by one, the whole waiting room is moving around inside of me.

Now they know the weight of my love.

Troy James Weaver is the author of *Witchita Stories*, *Temporal*, *Visions*, and *Marigold*. His stories have been published widely online and in print. He lives in Wichita, Kansas with his wife and dogs.

Jelly fish
Cheppup
Smoke love
Spring formal

CPSIA information can be obtained
at www.ICGtesting.com
Printed in the USA
LVHW110828060120
642628LV00004B/589/P